IVAN

by Marcus Crouch
illustrated by Bob Dewar

Oxford

Oxford University Press, Walton Street, Oxford OX2 6DP
Oxford   New York   Toronto
Delhi   Bombay   Calcutta   Madras   Karachi
Petaling Jaya   Singapore   Hong Kong   Tokyo
Nairobi   Dar es Salaam   Cape Town
Melbourne   Auckland

and associated companies in
Berlin   Ibadan

Oxford is a trade mark of Oxford University Press

British Library Cataloguing in Publication Data
Crouch, Marcus
Ivan. — (Oxford myths & legends).
I. Title   II. Dewar, Bob
823'.914 [J]   PZ7
ISBN 0-19-274135-7

Library of Congress Catalog Card Number 88–043217

Printed in Hong Kong

For David Davis
('David' of BBC Children's Hour)
with affection and gratitude

Contents

Ivan Lie-On-The-Stove

THERE he is. Just look at the idle good-for-nothing, dozing his life away on that warm stove.

Ivan is his name: Simple Ivan, Ivan the Fool, Daft Ivan or, if you are feeling kind, Ivan the Innocent. He is the youngest son. His big brothers go out to work; he stays at home taking care of his poor tired body and his delicate brain. He is saving his energies for a day that may never come.

You will always find an Ivan in Holy Russia. He was there when fierce tribes fought each other across the wide plains. He was around when tribal chiefs and kings brought a kind of peace to the land. He was a part of the Russia the Tsars ruled. I daresay you can find him still in distant corners of the country now that there are Soviets instead of Tsars.

Ivan is stupid and lazy. He is also cunning and resourceful. He sometimes comes out on top when the clever folk have failed. He may not always win the Princess's hand and half the kingdom, but in less showy ways he often succeeds. For Ivan does not give up easily. He has a habit of keeping going in his own stolid way, long after the rest have lost heart.

The Russians have always had their Ivan to spin tales around, just as the English have their Jack and the Germans their Hans. Sometimes you will find that he is a Prince Ivan who has splendid adventures and wins a kingdom for himself. Mostly he is a peasant, a poor country lad who owns little except his native wits. Put upon, bullied and cheated by his betters, he will come bobbing up again when you think he must be finished. Ivan is the great survivor. Around his name have accumulated many stories, sad, funny, exciting, magical. A few of them are told in this book.

So let us go and look in on Ivan and his family. . . .

Ivan Gets It Wrong

THEY were just an ordinary family. Only the youngest son, Ivan, was different. He was a silly fellow. He spent most of his time lying on top of the stove, singing quietly to himself and doing no harm, if no good. It was when he climbed down off the stove that trouble started. One thing Ivan was good at: he could always find just the wrong things to say and do.

In spite of everything, his mother loved him dearly. She spent hours teaching him what words he should use and how he should behave, but all her efforts went to waste. A fool Ivan was and a fool he would remain.

One day he went stumbling out of the house and wandered into the barn. All the workers were there, threshing the corn. There was dust all over the place, and the peasants were hot, dirty and short-tempered.

'Good lads,' shouted Ivan. 'Keep at it. I hope you work for three whole days and get a mouthful of grain apiece for your pains.'

They all turned on him and whacked him with their flails till the dust flew and the fool shouted.

Home went Ivan. 'Mother,' he said, 'they've been knocking a little chap about something terrible.'

'Have they, son? Who was it? Was it you?'

Ivan nodded sadly.

'What happened?'

Ivan told his story. 'Silly boy!' said his mother. 'You ought to have said: "Bravo! you're doing a fine job. Do as much every day."'

A day or two later Ivan went out into the village, and he met a funeral procession. Six strong men sweated under the weight of the coffin, and everyone was weeping and howling.

'Well done!' called Ivan. 'You're doing a fine job. Do as much every day.'

The strong bearers put down the coffin carefully. Then they turned on Ivan and punched him till his head rang.

Ivan went home crying and told his mother. She said: 'Poor silly boy! You should have said: "Rest in peace."'

Next time he went out he came upon a wedding. Everyone was dressed in fine clothes and they danced and sang.

Ivan said in his loudest voice: 'Rest in peace, poor sorrowful ones.'

The bridegroom climbed down from his cart and punched Ivan on the nose. Then the groomsman blacked his eye.

'What happened this time?' said Ivan's mother. 'Why, you poor lad, you should have joined in the fun and played your pipe.'

A few days later one of the cottages caught fire. Everyone ran to help put it out. They shouted and swore, dragged down the thatch, and threw water into the flames. Ivan ran too. He had brought his little pipe with him, and he took it out and played a merry tune, jigging in time with the music and laughing fit to burst his sides. Not for long! The fire-fighters took time off to beat him up and throw him into the duck-pond.

'What a boy you are!' said his mother. 'Why didn't you get a bucket of water and help put the fire out?'

Later that week the villagers held a feast. They lit a huge fire, and they were roasting a pig when Ivan came strolling along. He ran to find a bucket, filled it with water, and put the fire out with one bold throw.

Guess what happened to him! Yes, he came home again, groaning and weeping and covered with bruises.

'There's no help for it,' said his mother. 'From now on you stay at home.' And there he stopped and never once did he dare poke his nose outside the back gate.

Daydreams

Ivan's Master imagined that the lad was busy ploughing, but as usual he had stopped the plough and begun to dream.

He noticed a hare standing in the tall grass, and said to himself: 'What luck! I'll catch that hare. He should fetch a good price in the market. With the money I'll buy a young sow. Soon she will have a dozen piglets. I'll feed them all up, and they too will have litters of a dozen apiece. Then I'll slaughter the lot and sell the meat. That will bring me in enough to get married. Before long my wife will have two strong sons. I'll call them Vasha and Vanka. They will grow up and work for me. All I will have to do is sit in the porch in the sun, shouting at them. "Take it easy, boys," I'll say. "Care for those horses and they will take care of you. No need to whip them like that. It's easy to see you weren't born hard-up."'

Ivan waved his arms as he shouted at his sons. The hare took fright and ran off. And with the hare went Ivan's fine sons, his pretty wife, one hundred and fifty-six piglets, and one fat sow.

There's Plenty of Fish in the Trees

Not all Ivans were silly. Here is a story of one who had his head on the right way round.

Ivan had a wife who could never keep quiet. Tell her a secret and be sure all her gossips would know it before dinner. He did his best to cure her of her habit, but in vain; her tongue just went on flapping like washing on the line.

One day Ivan was working in the fields and his spade hit something hard. He felt around with his hands and found that he had struck a chest full of gold coins. He took it home and showed it to his wife.

'Our fortune's made,' he said. 'But we must be very careful. If the Master hears about it he will surely claim the treasure for himself. After all, it was buried on his land.'

They thought carefully about where they should hide the gold, and the wife said they should dig a hole in the floor. This is what they did, and Ivan smoothed the surface so that no signs of the treasure were to be seen.

'Now, my love, whatever you do, say no word of this to one living soul,' said Ivan. 'If a whisper of this reaches the Master's ears we shall be poor again, and he will have me whipped into the bargain.'

'Trust me,' said his wife. 'You know I always keep your secrets safe.'

Ivan knew no such thing. He waited until his wife was fast asleep; then he got up, dug up the gold and buried it in the barn, under a great heap of dung.

Next morning he said to his wife: 'Tomorrow we must go into the woods to catch fish.'

'Fish in the woods?' she said. 'I never knew that is where you catch them.'

'Why, of course; it's much the best place.' And Ivan kept his face very serious indeed.

While his wife was at the market, he took some fish that he had caught a day or two earlier, together with a dead hare and a basket full of stale cakes from the baker's, and he took them into the woods. When he came home he was empty-handed.

After they had eaten next morning Ivan took his wife by the hand and they walked to the woods together. Very soon she found a pike dangling from a tree. Next she found a perch and two roaches. She was even more surprised when she came upon a tree which was growing cakes.

'Look, husband,' she said. 'Cakes on a tree!'

'Of course,' he said, 'everyone knows that's where they grow.'

Now Ivan went down to the river and pulled in his line. On the hook there was a hare.

'Goodness me!' said the wife. 'Just fancy, hare in the river.'

'Quite a good one, too,' said Ivan calmly. 'Usually they are only half that size.'

He unhooked the hare and put it in his bag. Then they went home with the day's catch. They ate a good dinner that night.

By now the wife's wagging tongue had made sure that all the village knew about Ivan's treasure. Very soon the news reached the ears of the

Master in his big house. He sent for Ivan. The man went to the house, and he took his good wife with him.

'What is this I hear?' said the Master gravely. 'Have you found treasure on my land and not reported it to me?'

'It's just idle gossip,' said Ivan. 'There's not a word of truth in it.'

'But your own wife says it is true.'

'Oh, she's a crazy woman,' said Ivan. 'You can never believe a word she says.'

'That's not true,' said the wife. 'You know very well that you brought the treasure home.'

'When was that?'

'Why, it was the day before we caught fish in the woods.'

'What is this?' said the Master. 'Fish in the woods?'

'Yes, Master,' said the wife eagerly. 'And the very same day we picked cakes off the trees. There were lots of them. Then on the way home my man fished a fat hare out of the river.'

'Take her home,' said the Master to Ivan. 'You are right. She *is* a crazy woman.'

Still, the Master was no fool. He sent his men to the cottage when Ivan was out. They dug up the floor and searched high and low, but no treasure could they find. Ivan spent it coin by coin in the market, and it kept them in comfort for many years.

Big Ivan and Little Ivan

THERE were two brothers. They were more or less equal in theight, but people always called them Big Ivan and Little Ivan. Big Ivan was very rich. Everything always went well with him. When he worked his land you might say that the clods of earth turned up by his plough were as good as gold. As for Little Ivan the clods remained earth and even the earth would not grow much for him. His wife and children went hungry, while Big Ivan and his family grew fat.

One day Little Ivan's cottage was so bare that there was not one scrap to put on the table for dinner. He said to his wife: 'It's no use. I have done what I can. Now I must go to my brother and beg for help. Surely he will help me out for the sake of our mother's memory.'

So he went and humbled himself before his brother. Big Ivan stared at him and said: 'I'm not one to give charity. It is bad for the giver and no good for the one who takes. Work for me for a week and I will reward you.'

For one long week Little Ivan worked in his brother's house, carrying water, cutting and carrying wood, lighting fires, sweeping dirt from house and yard. He took no rest for a single minute of the day. His rich brother watched him and said nothing. When the week was up Big Ivan went to his store-room and came back with a loaf of bread. 'Here. Take this for your wages,' he said.

Little Ivan bowed to the ground. 'Thank you, kind brother,' he said.

'Now be off home,' said Big Ivan. 'But wait a moment. You can come tomorrow and bring your wife with you. It is my birthday, and I am having a feast. You shall be my guest.'

'I can't do that,' said Little Ivan. 'Just look at me. I haven't any fine clothes. What I have been wearing to do your work is all I own. What would I look like beside your fine rich friends? And my poor wife is no better off.'

'Never mind about that. Come. There will be a place for both of you.'

Little Ivan went home and gave his wife the loaf. 'Here's something for dinner. What is more, we are invited to a feast tomorrow.'

'What feast? Who would invite the likes of us to anything?'

'It is my kind brother. It is his birthday, and we are to eat with the best folk in town.'

Next day they got up early, and cleaned themselves as best they could. Then, in their shabby clothes, they walked to Big Ivan's house. They wished him a happy birthday and then went and sat humbly in a corner. Many people were there already, dressed in their finest clothes. They were all talking together, and they took no notice of Little Ivan and his wife. Food was brought in, rich dishes that smelt lovely and made Little Ivan's mouth water. Servants handed it round, but they quite forgot to serve the couple in the dark corner, so all Little Ivan and his wife enjoyed was the smell.

The feast was over at last. The guests stood up and went to thank Big Ivan for his generosity. Little Ivan did the same. Then they all left the house and went on their way, the well-fed guests singing noisily. Some of them could hardly walk, for those who hadn't eaten too much had certainly taken too much strong drink.

Little Ivan had no such difficulties. His belly was as empty as when he arrived at the feast and his head was quite clear. Still, it troubled him

that he and his wife were not sharing in the jollity. He said to her: 'Shall we sing too?'

'Don't be a fool,' said his loving wife. 'What have we got to sing about? All these drunken wretches are full of good food, and we have eaten nothing.'

Little Ivan said: 'It doesn't seem right creeping home in silence. After all we did go to my brother's feast. If we don't go home singing people will think we haven't enjoyed ourselves.'

'Please yourself. Sing if you must. I certainly won't.'

So Little Ivan lifted up his voice in song. After a few notes he stopped. It seemed to him that there were two people singing.

'Was that you joining in after all?' he said.

'Of course not. I'm in no mood for singing.'

Little Ivan started again, and sure enough he heard a weak little voice joining in with him. He peered into the dark night and saw a faint shadow of a figure standing near him.

'Who's there?' he said.

'I am your Bad Luck,' said the thin voice. 'I am never very far away from you.'

'Come on home then.'

'I'm coming,' said Bad Luck. 'I promise I won't ever desert you.'

Next evening Bad Luck asked Little Ivan to go to the inn with him for a drink.

'I've no money,' said Little Ivan.

'You don't need money. See that sheepskin hanging by the door. You won't need that again before winter. Take it to the inn. The innkeeper will surely let you have all the drink you want for that.'

So off they went together to the inn and Little Ivan drank and drank until his belly was afloat. He staggered home, leaning on Bad Luck. Next morning he felt terrible. His head seemed to be split in two. Bad Luck was not much better. 'We'll just have to go back and drink until we feel better,' said Bad Luck.

'What's the use? All my money went last night.'

'That's all right,' said Bad Luck. 'You have a good cart standing in the barn. That should be worth quite a lot of drink.'

So they dragged the cart to the inn and drank it away before

18

midnight. So it went on for a week, and every night one of Little Ivan's poor possessions turned itself miraculously into strong drink. When everything movable had gone he raised money on his house. That lasted a month. After that Bad Luck still urged him to go to the inn. 'I've nothing left,' moaned Little Ivan.

'What about your wife?' said Bad Luck. 'She has two dresses. She can only wear one at a time. Take the other to the inn tonight. It should be enough to give us just one more jolly evening.'

Next morning Little Ivan awoke in despair. Everything had gone. He had nothing left for drink, nothing to keep his own family alive.

Bad Luck saw his misery and said: 'Cheer up. I have an idea. Ask your neighbour to lend you his horse and cart for a day.'

'What for?'

'Never mind that. You will see.'

So Little Ivan went to his neighbour, and after some argument he got the use of a horse and cart. He and Bad Luck drove along until they came to a bit of open land. In the middle there was a big stone. 'Come on,' said Bad Luck. 'Get that side and I'll take this. Now heave!' And they pushed and pulled at the great stone until at last it fell on its side. In the hole Little Ivan saw a great heap of gold coins.

'Don't stand there staring,' said Bad Luck. 'Load it into the cart.'

They got busy, and in time the cart was heaped with gold. Little Ivan said: 'Jump into the hole and make sure we have got everything.'

Bad Luck crawled into the hole. When he was safely underground Little Ivan gave the stone a mighty shove, and it toppled back into its place, leaving Bad Luck buried.

'Just as well,' said Little Ivan. 'If I had you beside me, all this gold wouldn't keep us in drink for more than three months. Just rest quietly there until someone else needs you.'

So he drove home and hid the treasure in his house. He set about spending it quietly, just a little at a time, so that his neighbours only gradually realized that his fortunes were improving. He built himself a larger house, began to live in style, and before the year was out he was as well off as his brother, if not better.

One day he called on his brother. 'It's my birthday tomorrow,' he said. 'Come and share the feast with us, and bring your wife.'

'Feast?' said Big Ivan. 'When did you ever have money for a feast? Be off with you.'

'I mean it,' said Little Ivan. 'I am not doing badly these days. Come and see for yourself.'

So Big Ivan and his wife drove proudly to the brother's poor hut. But when they got there, where was the hut? A grand house stood there, better than their own.

Little Ivan had laid out a mighty feast, and his brother ate well of everything, and so did his wife. When they had eaten all they had room for, and more, Big Ivan said: 'You must tell me, brother. How is it that you have done so well for yourself?'

Little Ivan had drunk too much and could put no guard on his tongue. Before long he had told his brother the whole story, right up to the day when he had left Bad Luck buried under the stone.

Big Ivan went home full of food and envy. He lay awake all night, tormented with thoughts of his brother's wealth and happiness. How he hated him for it! By morning he had thought of a plan. He would go to the stone and let Bad Luck out, so that he could return to his brother and ruin him. When the little brother was penniless Big Ivan could hold up his head in pride once more.

As soon as he could he went to the open land where the great stone stood. It was still loose where Little Ivan had shifted it, and he had no great difficulty in heaving it on to its side. He bent down to see what lay below, and Bad Luck leapt out and clung to his back.

'Got you!' screamed Bad Luck. 'You thought you had got rid of me, didn't you? Now I'm free, and I promise I'll never leave you again as long as you live.'

'It wasn't me,' said Big Ivan. 'It was my wicked brother. I came here to set you free.'

'Liar!' said Bad Luck. 'You tricked me once, but you won't do it again. I'm here to stay.'

And stay he did. Big Ivan's fortune began to shrink, just as his brother's poor possessions had, until nothing but poverty lay before him.

'I must get rid of this pest,' he said to himself. He thought for a long time, then he went to his yard and cut himself two sharp wooden stakes.

He took a new cart-wheel and pushed one of the stakes into the hub, point inwards. Then he went indoors and found Bad Luck lying in bed.

'Why are you so lazy these days?' he said. 'Stir yourself, Bad Luck. Come into the yard and we will play a game.'

They went to the yard. 'I know,' said Big Ivan. 'Let's play hide-and-seek. I'll hide first.'

Bad Luck found him at once. He was pleased with himself and boasted: 'It's my turn now. You won't find me. I can squeeze into any hole, however small.'

'I bet you couldn't get in there,' said Big Ivan, and he pointed to the hub of the wheel.

'That's easy,' said Bad Luck. He made himself very small and crawled into the hub. Big Ivan picked up the second stake and rammed it hard into the hub. Then he picked up the wheel and threw it into the river.

Without Bad Luck he soon became as rich as his brother again and twice as proud.

Did everyone live happily ever after? Well, wooden wheels float. I am sure it wasn't long before some poor wretch let Bad Luck out of his prison and soon regretted that kindness. You don't get rid of Bad Luck easily.

Sharing the Reward

IT had been a splendid parade. A thousand soldiers, got up in their smartest uniforms, had taken part, and the king himself had ridden at their head on his white charger. Now the troops had been dismissed, and the king rode back to his palace. When he got there he discovered that a ring had fallen off his finger during the day. Greatly upset, because it was a ring which he valued for a special reason, the king gave orders that anyone who found it would have a big reward.

On his way back to barracks Private Ivan noticed something shining in the road. Bending down he saw that it was a gold ring. He picked it up and went on his way, wondering at his own good luck. Luck was not something that often came his way. Mostly he was kicked and cursed by his officers and none too kindly treated by his mates.

In the barrack room the news had already got about. The king had lost a ring, and the finder would be richly rewarded.

'Here's a problem,' thought Ivan. 'If I keep the ring for myself it may one day be traced back to the king, and then I shall be in real trouble. On the other hand if I do the proper thing and report the find to the officer he is sure to stick to the reward himself and I shan't get a smell of it.'

Greatly daring, Ivan decided that he would break all the rules and go straight to the king. That, it turned out, was not easy. When he got to the palace he was stopped by the officer of the guard. 'What do you want, soldier?' said this great man.

'I have business with the king, sir.'

'And what kind of business would the king have with you, little man?'

'I've found his ring, if you please, sir.'

'Have you now?' said the officer.

'Well, without my say-so you won't get anywhere near the king, so you and I had better make a bargain. If I give the order to let you through you must give me half the reward. Is it a deal?'

Ivan did not like this idea one bit, but what could he do? He was only a poor private soldier, and without the officer's help he would get nowhere. So he said: 'Very well. But I want it down in black and white. Write me a note saying that half the reward is for you and half for me.'

'All right,' said the officer impatiently, and he hurriedly scribbled a note. Then he led Ivan to the king. 'This young soldier has some news for you, Your Majesty,' he said.

The king was delighted to see his ring again. 'Bravo, soldier,' he said. 'You have done well. Now for your reward. What would you say to one hundred gold pounds?'

'Oh no, Your Majesty, that's not for the likes of me. I'm just a poor common soldier. What would I do with all that money? No, what us privates usually get given is a couple of hundred lashes from the sergeant-major. That will be good enough for me.'

'You are a strange fellow and no mistake,' said the king. 'However, if you think that is what you deserve, that is what you must have,' and he sent for the executioner to carry out the punishment there and then.

Ivan began to strip. As he took off his tunic he let the officer's note drop to the floor.

'What is that?' said the king.

'It's an agreement, Your Majesty. It says that any reward I get today must go half to me and half to the officer of the guard.'

The king laughed, and said: 'I think we ought to give the officer his half first, don't you? After all, he is senior to you.'

So the wretched officer was ordered to take off his shirt, and a hundred lashes were laid on vigorously. The executioner had nearly finished when Ivan said to the king: 'Your Majesty, that officer is more in need than I am. Don't you think he should have my half too? I will gladly give him my share.'

'That is kind of you,' said the king. 'I hope he appreciates your generosity,' and he ordered the executioner to lay on the second hundred strokes. By the time he had finished the officer had scarcely strength enough to crawl through the door.

'Now,' said the king, 'so far justice has been done. Let us continue to give it with an open hand. It seems to me that you are too smart to go on being a private soldier. Take your discharge from the army and two hundred pounds to help you on your way.'

And laughing heartily the king dismissed Ivan to his home.

Three Sisters

PRINCE Ivan had everything a man could possibly want. He was rich, handsome and wise. Everyone in the kingdom loved him, especially the girls. And yet he wasn't contented. He longed for something else, he knew not what. Somewhere in the world, he believed, he would find what he needed to complete his happiness.

After much pondering Prince Ivan went to his father the king and asked his blessing. He must go out and see the world. And so he began his journey.

He travelled many weary miles, saw strange countries, and had great adventures. At last he came one day to a fine palace. Three beautiful young women were sitting by the door. They were sisters and they were deep in conversation. Prince Ivan stopped to listen, and this is what he heard.

'If Prince Ivan married me,' said the eldest girl, 'I would spin him a shirt so fine that it would sit upon his back no heavier than a spider's web.'

The middle sister said: 'If Prince Ivan married me I would sew him a coat of gold and silver and precious gems and he would shine like the stars.'

'Oh dear!' said the youngest sister. 'I wish I was clever like you. But if Prince Ivan married me and loved me like his own soul I would give him three sons as strong as bears and as swift as eagles. Each would have the sun on his forehead and stars on his sides.'

The prince knew that his search was at an end. He returned home at once and told his father that he wished to be married. The king gave his consent, and Prince Ivan married the youngest sister. They were very happy together, but the elder sisters were filled with rage and envy, which they took good care to hide. To the world they showed bright faces and they hid the blackness of their hearts.

In time the young princess had a baby boy. The sisters nursed her with tender care, but when Prince Ivan came hurrying to see his son they showed him not a child with the sun on his forehead and stars on his sides but a baby kitten.

The prince was sad and angry, but he hoped for better things next time. Again the sisters tended the princess, and this time they showed Prince Ivan a new-born puppy. For all his grief the prince still loved his wife dearly, and he was sure that the third time would be better.

Again the princess took to her room; her sisters fussed over her and showed her every kind of tenderness. Then Prince Ivan came to the nursery, full of eager hopefulness, but this time the sisters showed him not a kitten or a puppy or a baby with the sun on his forehead and stars on his sides, but just a plain ordinary baby boy.

At this last blow the prince lost heart. His wife had failed him three times, and he no longer hoped for an heir. He ordered the princess to be brought before the judges to answer for her failures. The judges listened carefully to the evidence. Some thought that the princess ought to be put to death, others that she should be sent back to her father in disgrace. At last the chief judge gave his verdict. She should be put into a barrel with her baby son, and the barrel should be nailed up and thrown into the sea, to float where it would.

So it was done. Prince Ivan took to his room and stayed there, deep in misery. In vain the elder sisters tried to coax him, pretending to be full of pity and understanding. The prince was not to be comforted.

Meanwhile the barrel tossed on the ocean, battered by storms and scorched by the hot sun. After a few days the waves set it down on the shore of a strange land. It lay there for a while, then suddenly it burst open. Out came the princess and with her a tall young man, strong and beautiful. It was the baby, who had grown as much in an hour as most children grow in a year.

The magic that made him grow had given him strange powers. He knelt on the sand and prayed aloud:

'By the power of God and man
By the strength of sun and sea
Lift the princess and me
To the home of Prince Ivan.'

At once a great wind arose. It lifted the young man and the princess and carried them back over the sea, setting them down gently in the garden behind Prince Ivan's palace.

In a forgotten corner of the garden they saw a little house from which came the sound of music and laughter. They went inside, and there they found three tall boys, each with the sun on his forehead and stars on his sides.

The princess knew them for her own, and they ran to her with many kisses and wondering questions. When all had been told the three young princes took to their hearts the other young man (whom the wicked sisters had cruelly stolen and put in the place of the youngest) and swore that he would be their brother in all things.

There they all stayed, waiting for the day when it would be safe for them to declare themselves to the prince their father. Time did not hang heavily on them, for they were young and happy in their comradeship, and their mother's love kept them in good spirits.

One day a party of travellers came that way. They were tired and hungry, and the young brothers took them in and gave them all they needed. After they had eaten and slept the travellers went on their way and came to the palace.

Prince Ivan sat at the door, deep in sad thoughts.

'Greetings, friends,' he said to the travellers. 'Sit down and tell me what you have seen in this wide and weary world.'

'Wide it certainly is, Your Highness,' they said, 'but never weary. We have seen many strange things, wild animals and more terrible wild men. But the greatest wonder we have seen is here in your own garden. There live no fewer than three beautiful young boys with the sun on their foreheads and stars on their sides, and their mother with them who is more beautiful even than they.'

Prince Ivan wasted no time. He strode into his garden and came to the garden house, from which came the sounds of music and laughter. He opened the door and saw his fine sons and their lovely mother.

He knelt before her to beg forgiveness, and then gave himself up to joy.

A Little Vixen

THE peasant and his goodwife had only one son, and he was no great blessing to them because, though good-hearted, he was so thick in the head that he could never get anything right. 'What are we to do with our Ivan?' said the wife one day, when the lad had done something especially silly. 'The only thing he's good at is eating, and we have barely enough food to keep the two of us alive. Let's get rid of him. It's high time he learnt to make his own way in the world.'

So they gave young Ivan their blessing. With it he also took a half-ruined hut in the forest, a cock and five hens (don't forget the hens—they are important) and a horse. Did I say horse? Well, it was not so much a horse as a wretched old broken-backed nag, good for nothing but chewing hay, and he had few teeth left to help him do that.

Ivan rode to the forest and let out his cock and hens to scratch for whatever food they could find. Ivan went to bed. Next morning he thought that he had better go hunting for his dinner. When he had gone out of sight of the hut someone appeared. This was a little vixen who had watched with interest the arrival of her new neighbour. She went sniffing around and soon picked up the smell of tasty hen. In no time she had tracked down a hen and killed it, and wasn't it good to eat? When Ivan came back in the evening he counted his hens and found one missing. 'Poor creature!' he thought. 'I suppose she must have many enemies in the forest. Perhaps a hawk took her.'

When he went off hunting next day he happened to meet the little vixen.

'Where are you going, Ivan?' she asked.

'I am a-hunting, little vixen.'

'Good luck to you then.' And the vixen ran off. And where do you think she went? Why, straight to Ivan's hut, and there she killed a second hen and ate it. It tasted better than the first.

Ivan came home. Another hen missing! Could it possibly be that pretty little vixen who was to blame? On the third day he shut up the cock and the three remaining hens and barred door and window. Then he went hunting.

Soon he met the little vixen.

'Where are you off to this fine day, Ivan?'

'I'm going hunting, little vixen.'

'Good luck to you.'

Off ran the vixen, but Ivan turned back and followed her. He watched as she tried the door and the window and sniffed all around the hut. Then she climbed on to the roof and scrambled down the chimney. Ivan ran inside in time to catch her.

'So this is the thief,' he said. 'Good morning, little vixen. So you were going hunting too, were you? It seems that I have caught you.'

'Don't hurt me, Ivan,' said the little vixen. 'That won't do you any good. Let me live and I can be useful to you. You take care of me, and I will get you a rich wife.'

Ivan sat down to think, and he wasn't very good at that exercise. After a while he said: 'Very well. I'll give you a chance, but if you fail me I'll surely cut off that fine tail of yours.'

'You won't regret this,' said the little vixen. 'Now if I am to find you a wife I shall have to keep fit and well and have plenty to eat. For a start let me have another of your hens.'

So Ivan killed his third hen and gave it to her. She ate greedily, then sat a while washing her face. After some thought she said: 'I have it. You shall marry the Tsar's daughter. They tell me she is fairly good-looking, and her father will surely give her enough money for two.'

'How can a fellow like me marry a princess?'

'Never you mind. That's my worry, not yours.'

The little vixen ran off and made her way to the Tsar's palace. She went in and bowed before the Tsar. 'Greetings, Your Greatness.'

'Greetings to you too, little vixen,' said the Tsar. 'What tales of scandal have you brought me today?'

'No scandal; I am here on a matter of state. I come to make a marriage. You have the bride. I have the groom, and a rich and handsome one too. His name is Ivan Getrichquick.'

'Where is he then? Can't he speak for himself?'

'Oh, he is far too busy just now,' said the little vixen. 'He is king of the animals and he has many subjects to care for.'

'What kind of bridegroom are you offering me? Very well, tell him to send me forty times forty wolves, and then I will consider his proposal.'

The little vixen went back to the forest, found an open clearing and began to roll over and over on her back. A big grey wolf came up and stared at her, and said: 'What's up with you, neighbour? You look as if you have come from a good feast.'

'Oh dear!' said the little vixen. 'I do wish I hadn't eaten quite so much. But the Tsar was so pressing. He wouldn't let me refuse a single mouthful. I wonder you weren't there too, brother. All the other animals were invited.'

The wolf said: 'Little vixen, we have always been good friends. Won't you take me with you to the next feast?'

'I think I might manage that. But the Tsar won't be too pleased to see just a single wolf there. He likes to do things in style. Call up your tribe and be here tomorrow with forty times forty wolves, and I'll take you all.'

Sure enough, next day all the wolves were waiting, and the little vixen led them to the palace. 'Great Tsar!' she said. 'My master sends you the small gift you asked; forty times forty grey wolves.'

'This is well done,' said the Tsar. 'Now he can send me an equal number of bears.'

In just the same way the little vixen tricked the bears into coming to the palace, and they, like the wolves, went tamely into captivity.

'You have done very well, little vixen,' said the Tsar. 'But what use are all these wild beasts to me? I can't eat wolves, or train bears to run with my hunting dogs. Next time you must bring me forty times forty sables and ermine. At least they will give my family warm coats for the winter.'

The little vixen went home to Ivan's hut. 'Everything is going well,'

she said. 'Now you can kill the fourth hen. I have been working very hard and have a great appetite.'

So the fourth hen was eaten, and then the little vixen went back to the clearing in the forest and began rolling. An ermine came slinking by and said to her: 'Whatever is the matter, little vixen? Anyone might think you had the belly-ache.'

'So would you have if you had eaten such a feast as I have just had at the palace. The Tsar was most generous. He piled the tables high and all the animals gorged themselves.'

'If only I had been there,' said the ermine. 'It's not that I am a greedy eater, but I do enjoy fine company. I have always longed to go to Court. Couldn't you take me there, dear good vixen?'

'I am sure the Tsar would not think much of having a single ermine at his feast. He likes big numbers. Now, if you could round up, say, forty times forty of your family and your cousins the sables, then I dare say I could get you into the palace.'

So it was that next day forty times forty little animals, all in the richest of fur coats, presented themselves before the Tsar. 'Here they are, Your Greatness, just as you ordered,' said the little vixen, bowing to the ground.

'That is well done,' said the Tsar. 'Your Master has met all my demands. I accept him as my son-in-law. Tell him to come here himself tomorrow. It is high time he had a look at his bride.'

On the following morning the little vixen came alone to the palace. 'My Master sends his regrets, Your Greatness,' she said. 'He would dearly have liked to come himself, but he is over his ears in work today. It is his day for the Treasury, and he will be hard at work till nightfall counting his gold.'

'I am sorry he has so much to do,' said the Tsar. 'It would not take me all day to count *my* gold. I hope we may enjoy his company tomorrow. My daughter grows impatient.'

Home went the little vixen. Poor Ivan was lying in the hut, starving. Since the vixen had been gobbling his hens he had eaten nothing. There was just one hen and the cock left, but he had been reluctant to kill them, for they were all he had left except the horse, and that was too old to make a meal for even a starving man.

'Get up! Get up!' said the little vixen. 'This is your big day. The Tsar is quite won over and is waiting to greet you as his daughter's groom.'

'Are you crazy?' said Ivan. 'How can I go before the Tsar dressed in these rags?'

'Don't argue. Just saddle your horse and away! Leave all the little details to me. But before we go I'll just have that last hen, and the cock too. You won't be needing them any more.'

Ivan was not at all happy about the way things were going, but by now he was used to doing what the vixen told him. He whistled up his wretched horse, threw an old blanket over its bent back, and scrambled up. They went shambling off towards the palace, while the little vixen ran beside them. They came to a little wooden bridge over a river.

'Get down,' said the little vixen. 'Now push hard on the supports of the bridge.'

Ivan did as he was told. The bridge was old and rotten, and it soon went crashing, splashing into the water.

'Now jump into the river.'

The little vixen then ran to the palace and rushed in, shouting: 'Help! Help! What a disaster!'

'Why, whatever has happened?' said the Tsar.

'My poor master! He was riding to visit you, his horse laden with rich gifts, when one of your bridges broke down under him. He is surely drowned.'

At once the Tsar called his servants and told them to run to the bridge, taking fine clothes with them. When they got there they found Ivan lying on the bank. All his ragged clothes had been washed away in the stream, and of his great treasure there was no sign. They picked him up, pummelled him to shake out all the water, and then dressed him in some of the Tsar's own robes.

Back at the palace the Tsar welcomed him joyfully, and ordered that the wedding should take place at once, before anything else could happen to the bridegroom.

So that was that. Ivan married the princess. He lay about all day, singing to himself, eating all he wanted, adored by his wife and admired by his royal father-in-law.

And what about the little vixen? Well, she enjoyed the life of the Court for a time, spoiled and pampered by everyone, petted by the ladies, fed titbits by the gentlemen. It was very nice, but after all no wild creature wants to be a ladies' pet for ever. It wasn't long before she found herself missing the wild wood and the thrill of catching her own food. So she slipped quietly away one day and went back to her own ways.

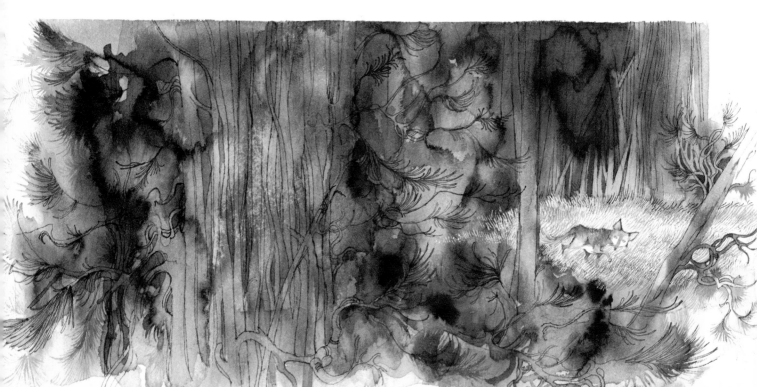

Little Bear

THERE was a farmer who was better off than most of his neighbours, but he counted himself poor because he had no son to take on the farm when he was old.

One day his wife went into the woods to look for mushrooms. She wandered into the deepest part of the forest, and a bear came lumbering out of the trees and carried her off to his cave. When she did not come home her husband searched everywhere for her but found only the scarf she had been wearing around her head. There was no other sign of her. Time went by, and at last he was sure that she was dead.

His wife lived on in the bear's den. Life was hard, but she made the best of it. Besides, the bear, even if it was only a dumb brute, was gentle with her and made sure that she did not go short of food. The time came when she gave birth to a baby. He was a strange creature; down to the waist he was like any other baby boy, but from the waist down he was a bear. Queer he might be, but he was his mother's son and she loved him. She named him Ivanko.

Years passed. Ivanko grew into a fine strong boy. The bear was proud of him, but his mother had told him about the village where she lived and he longed to see his rightful home.

The chance came when the bear went on a long journey to find a beehive in order to rob it of its honey. While he was away the woman and her son ran away and at last they came to their home. The farmer was greatly pleased to see his wife. Then he turned to the boy and said: 'Whatever is this odd creature?'

His wife told him the whole story, and the farmer decided that he had better treat the strange boy as his own son. 'Well, Little Bear,' he said. 'This is your home, but you must work for your keep. We will have mutton for dinner today to celebrate your homecoming. Take this knife and go and slaughter a sheep.'

'Which one shall I kill, Daddy?'

The farmer laughed and said jokingly: 'Oh, whichever one stares at you.'

Ivanko went into the yard and looked at the flock of sheep. When he appeared they all turned round together, staring at him and baaing loudly at the strange sight. He grabbed the first one and slit its throat, then went on to the next and the next until he had killed the whole flock.

The wretched sheep made a great noise and the farmer came out to see what was the matter. 'You idiot!' he shouted. 'I told you to slaughter a sheep for dinner, not to wipe out the whole flock.'

'But they all stared at me, Daddy,' said Ivanko.

'Well, you are a bright boy and no mistake,' said the farmer. 'However, what is done is done. Drag all the bodies into the barn. You can keep watch tonight. Guard the door well. There are thieves about.'

Night fell. Little Bear sat on the ground outside the barn, guarding the door. It came on to rain. He put up with it at first, but soon the rain came pelting down, drenching him to the skin. Ivanko could stand it no longer. He took the barn door off its hinges and struggled with it into the kitchen. He put it down on the floor and lay down on it to sleep.

Later in the night thieves came. They found the barn wide open and cleared it of everything: meat, farm tools, the lot.

In the morning the farmer got up and went to look at his barn. He

40

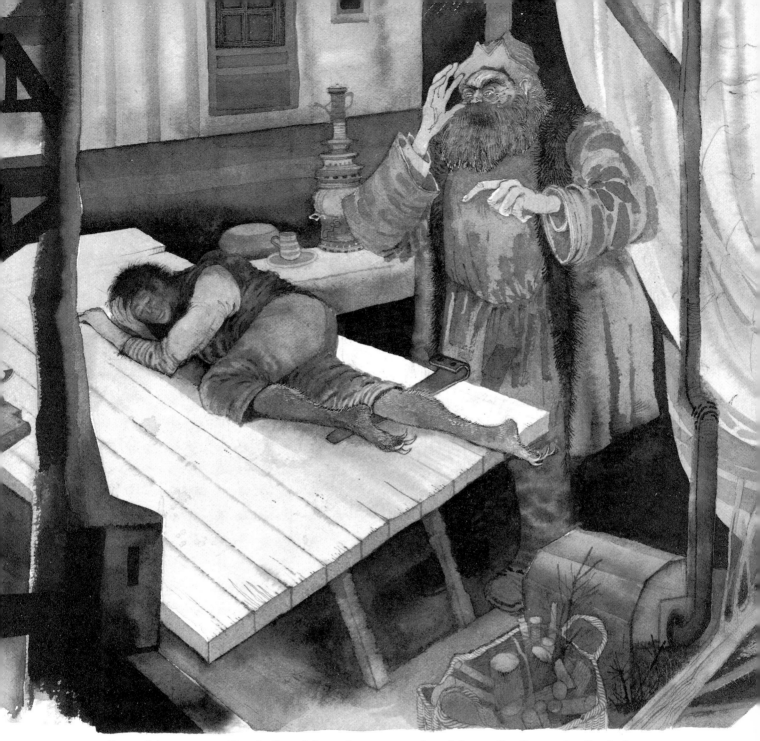

found it empty. Such few bits of meat as the thieves had overlooked the dogs had eaten. Where was the guard? The farmer found him sleeping peacefully on the barn door in the kitchen. 'You young rogue!' he shouted. 'Didn't I tell you to keep watch all night?'

'I did what you told me, Daddy,' said Ivanko. 'You said to guard the door, and I kept it safe all night.'

'What am I to do with this idiot?' thought the farmer. 'If he carries on like this I shall be broke in a month. I'll have to keep him out of harm's way.'

41

There was a lake nearby with a wide sandy shore. The farmer sent Ivanko there and told him to wind ropes of sand. This useless task would certainly do no good, but at least Little Bear could hardly do any harm. So Ivanko sat on the sand and tried to weave ropes out of it. He sang happily to himself as he worked.

Now this lake was the home of many devils who were causing a great deal of trouble in the neighbourhood. One of the younger devils came out of the water and said: 'What are you up to, Little Bear?'

'I'm making ropes. When I have finished I am going to thrash the water with my rope and torment all you devils. Here you are, living in our lake and you never pay a penny in rent.'

'Hold on, Little Bear,' said the young devil. 'I must ask my grandad what to do about this,' and he went 'plop' into the water.

He was back in a moment. 'Listen, Little Bear,' he said. 'My grandad will make a bargain with you. If you can run faster than me, we'll pay the rent. If I beat you, we'll drag you down into the water and drown you.'

'You look as if you could shift,' said Ivanko. 'But I don't care much for your chances. Why, my little boy was only born yesterday and even he could beat you. Perhaps you would rather race with him. There he is, hiding behind that bush.'

At that moment, a hare ran out and was out of sight in a few seconds. The little devil ran after him, but he was never in the race at all.

'It's my turn now,' said Ivanko, 'but I warn you, devil; if you lose I shall wring your little neck.'

The devil gave a shrill squeal and jumped into the lake. He was back before long carrying with him a huge iron crutch which his grandaddy used to help him get around on the floor of the lake.

'Grandad says, if you can throw this crutch higher than I can, he'll pay the rent.'

'Right,' said Ivanko, 'you can go first this time.'

The little devil picked up the crutch and threw it nearly out of sight. It came down with a great thump and dug itself deeply into the ground.

'Your turn now,' said the devil.

Ivanko took hold of the crutch, but he could barely lift it. 'Hold on a

moment,' he said. 'Do you see that cloud? I'm going to throw the crutch on to it and we'll never see it again.'

'Don't do that. Grandad doesn't want to lose it.' And the devil grabbed the crutch and dived back into the water.

Next time he came out, he was leading a big horse. 'Grandad says, if you can carry this horse round the lake more times than I can he will pay the rent. If I win, into the lake you go.'

'That's a poor sort of test,' said Ivanko. 'Very well; let's see what you can do.'

The devil picked up the horse and set off around the lake. Ten times round he went, till his legs were giving way under him and sweat burst out of his ears.

'My turn,' said Ivanko. He jumped on the horse's back and went off at a brisk trot. Round and round the lake he rode, until the poor horse collapsed under him.

'Well, little devil,' he said; 'How did I do?'

'That's a queer way of carrying a horse, between your legs,' said the devil. 'I'm sure I couldn't have done that. I give you the victory. How much rent do we owe?

'You must fill my hat with gold, and then work as my servant for a year.'

Ivanko went to a place where miners had been digging a great hole. He cut the crown out of his hat, and put the hat upside-down over the hole. The little devil came out of the lake, carrying an armful of gold. Into the hat it went, and there was still room for more. Back and forth that devil went, sweating hotly, and still he couldn't fill the hat. He worked hard all day, and towards evening, just as the light was fading, the last load went into the hat and stayed there. The job was done. The little devil dropped to the ground, panting.

Ivanko went and got a cart and piled it high with gold. Then he said to the little devil: 'Get up. There's work to be done.' He made the poor devil haul the cart to his father's farm. Ivanko banged on the door. When the farmer opened it Ivanko said: 'Cheer up, Daddy. Here's a servant to work for you, and some gold too. Not a bad day's work for a Little Bear, is it?'

Ivan the Unlucky

EVERYONE called him Ivan the Unlucky, but was he? What do *you* think?

Ivan was left an orphan when his father, a rich and successful merchant, died. He was also left his father's fortune, and he at once set about spending it as quickly as possible. Drinking, gambling, jollity soon accounted for everything that it had taken his father a lifetime of care and hard work to build up. So, just a year after becoming a rich man, Ivan was penniless. Did that make him unlucky? Foolish rather than unlucky, I'd say.

Anyway, he went for a stroll through the town looking for work. A girl was sitting in the window of her father's shop embroidering a carpet. Her work was very beautiful, and so was she. Ivan walked by and glanced in the window. She saw him and at once found that she was in love. 'I must marry him,' she told her mother. Mother was no fool. Well she knew what kind of husband Ivan was likely to make, but her daughter had always been able to get her own way in most things, and she would no doubt do the same this time. Mother talked it over with her husband, a rich tradesman. 'The lad's little short of being an idiot,' she said, 'but then our daughter has always had more than her share of good luck. Perhaps she will share a little of it with him.'

So the parents agreed to the marriage. Ivan was pleased too. Marrying a rich wife, and a lucky one into the bargain, was better than working. The wedding took place without delay. The bride was very happy, but that did not mean that she stopped work. No, she enjoyed her embroidery, and she had an idea for keeping her new husband occupied. She made a very fine carpet and told Ivan to go out and sell it. 'It's worth every bit of twenty pounds,' she said. 'However, if you should find a wise man, exchange the carpet for his good advice.'

Ivan went out with the carpet over his shoulder. An old man saw him and called out: 'How much for the carpet?'

Ivan said: 'I'll take twenty pounds.'

'Done!' said the old man. 'Will you take it in cash, or will you have twenty pounds' worth of advice?'

Ivan remembered what his wife had told him, so he said: 'I'll have the advice.'

'Fear nothing but death.'

Ivan went home and told his wife what had happened. She nodded her head, and at once began work on another carpet. It was even better than the first. 'Here,' she said, 'this carpet is worth fifty pounds. See that you get that much for it, or a good piece of advice.'

In the market Ivan saw the old man again. 'How much this time?' said the old man. 'Fifty pounds, or the same in good advice,' said Ivan.

'I'll take it,' said the old man. 'Listen carefully. Think before you act. Don't lose your head, and don't make anyone else lose his.'

Ivan returned home and told his wife all about it. She just nodded.

It was not long before the wife's father and his brothers got ready for a trading venture overseas. They filled several ships with their goods. Ivan wanted his share of adventure, and he persuaded his new father-in-law to lend him the money to buy his own ship. He kissed his wife goodbye, and set sail for distant lands.

He had been sailing some days in company with the other ships when a great creature came up from the sea-bed and challenged them. The monster roared: 'There's an argument going on down below. I want a man of good judgement to come and settle it. There's no need to be afraid; I'll bring him back safely.'

The other merchants had no good opinion of Ivan's judgement. Indeed, they thought him no better than a fool. On the other hand they didn't fancy going down under the sea. They all said: 'Let Ivan go.'

Ivan was not at all happy about this. Then he remembered the old man's advice: 'Fear nothing but death.' So he said: 'I will go.'

The monster took him on its back, and dived deep down to the bottom of the sea. The king of the sea was sitting, gazing at three bars of metal: gold, silver, and iron. 'Good lad!' he said when Ivan arrived. 'Listen. I can't decide which is the most valuable of these metals. What do you think?'

'Well,' said Ivan, 'have you ever seen a warrior with a golden sword? Or a farmer with a silver plough? No, take iron everytime.'

'Well spoken!' said the sea-king. 'Thank you for your help. You will find a small reward when you get back to your ship.'

When Ivan got aboard again he found that the hold had been filled to the brim with precious stones.

His wife's uncles had not waited for him, so he sailed on after them. In time he caught up and they reached port together. Before they went ashore to sell their goods the merchants had a discussion about whose cargo was likely to prove most valuable.

'Mine is the best,' said Ivan.

'Don't be a fool,' said the others. 'How can it be best? You have only one ship, while we have dozens.'

What they had all wanted to be a quiet discussion finished up as a furious argument. Ivan wouldn't give way, and at last the others decided to ask the king to judge who was in the right.

The king looked at the merchants, all sober, mature men, and at Ivan, a boy who looked an idiot. 'There can't be much doubt,' he said, 'but I will be fair. Let me see samples of your wares.'

The merchants brought in fine cloth, beautiful silk scarves, beds made of pure gold inlaid with ivory. 'These are splendid,' said the king.

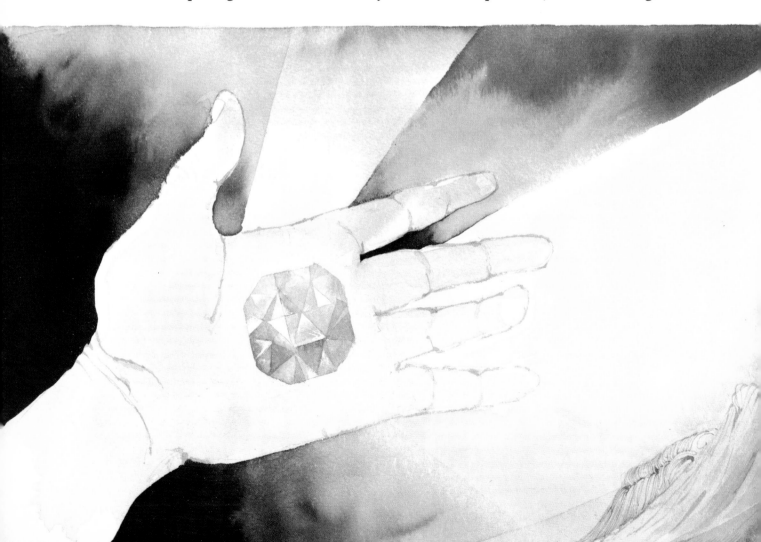

'Rarely have I seen such magnificent work. Now, young man, what have you to show?'

'Your Majesty, if you please, put curtains at your windows and make the room quite dark. I cannot show my wares in the light.'

The room was darkened. Ivan felt in his purse and pulled out a single precious stone. He held it on the palm of his hand and it lit the room as if the sun was shining there.

The king said: 'No one could better that. Go in peace, young man. Because your fellow traders have asked me for judgement, my ruling is this: they shall each pay you a quarter of the value of their cargoes.'

So Ivan the Unlucky turned out to be lucky indeed. He took his fortune, and went trading around the world. Time went by, ten years, fifteen. At last he thought that he had been away from his wife long enough. He set sail for home, rich beyond measure. Back on shore he ran to his house like a boy, full of eagerness to see his wife again.

He found his wife in bed, and two handsome young men were with her, laughing and talking. Ivan was filled with rage. He drew his sword and went to kill them all three. Then, far away in the depth of his memory, he heard the words of the old man: 'Think before you act. Don't lose your head, and don't make anyone else lose his.'

Ivan dropped his sword and walked forward. His wife saw him and leapt up with a cry of joy. 'You are back, my love!' Then she shook the two young men and said: 'Get up, children. Your father has come home.'

That's where we leave Ivan, with a great fortune, a lovely wife and fine twin sons. Not bad for an unlucky fellow!

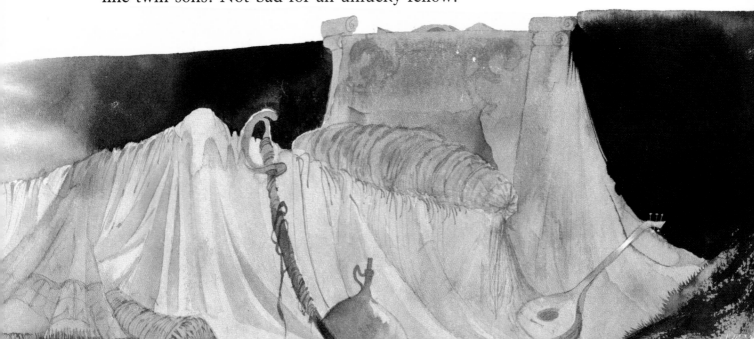

Ivan and the Bear

'FATHER,' said Ivan the Simpleton, 'I want to get married. Find me a wife.'

'It's not that easy, son. You don't just go out and pick up a wife on the corner of the road. You need money, and I have none.'

Ivan said: 'I want a wife. If you don't get me a wife I shall scream and shout and break the furniture. If you've got no money, sell something and get some. Sell the ox.'

Ivan was shouting so loudly that far off in his stall the ox heard him. He did not much care for the idea of being sold to the butcher, so he ran away into the woods.

'The ox has disappeared,' said the father. 'It can't be helped. You will just have to do without a wife.'

'Sell something else. Wring the cock's neck and bake him in a pie. You can surely sell that and get me a wife.'

Out on the dunghill the cock heard this, and he too made his way into the woods just as fast as he could scuttle.

'The cock has gone, son. It can't be helped. You must put off the wedding for a year or two.'

'I want a wife,' said Ivan. 'I want her now. Sell something else. Sell a sheep. The butcher will pay good money for that.'

In the meadow the sheep heard Ivan bellowing. Not waiting to hear more she ran away and joined her friends in the woods. There they built themselves a little hut and settled down to live happily together.

A bear who lived in the woods watched them at their work. It seemed to him that the three animals put together would make him at least one good meal, so he padded off to the hut and banged on the door. The cock saw him through the window, and flew up into the roof, flapping his wings vigorously and crowing: 'Where is he? I'll get him. I'll stamp on him. I'll chop him into little bits. Where did I put that knife? Fetch me that axe. Bears! I eat them before breakfast.'

The bear was scared out of his few wits. He turned and ran. He ran and ran, blundering into trees and tripping over roots. At last, what with the fright and the running, his heart could beat no longer. He dropped down and died.

Ivan was walking in the woods, muttering to himself: 'I want a wife. I will have a wife. I'll sell something, no matter what.' He tripped over something on the path, got up and found that it was a dead bear. He pulled out his knife and took the hide off very neatly. His father took the skin to market, and with the money Ivan was able to get himself a strong, healthy wife.

I suppose they lived happily ever after.

Three Brides for Three Brothers

THERE were three brothers. Two were much like you and me, neither clever nor stupid, industrious nor lazy. The youngest was as idle and silly as you could come across in a day's march. His name was Ivashko.

Father grew tired of having three big lads around the house. It was surely time that the two older boys at least found themselves wives and set up house on their own. As for Ivashko, he saw no hope of finding a wife for that one. There must be plenty of silly girls around, but not that silly!

So the eldest son was sent out to look for a bride. He walked about the village and saw no girl to his liking. He decided to try the next village. On the road he met a dragon.

'And where are you off to, my lad?' said the dragon.

'I'm looking for a wife, if you please, sir,' said the young man. 'So far I can't find one I fancy.'

'Come with me,' said the dragon. 'Let us see if you are fit to be married.'

He led the way till they came to a great stone standing by the road. The dragon said: 'Roll the stone over. Then we shall see if we can find a wife for you.'

Well, the eldest brother pushed and shoved, but he couldn't get that stone to move. The dragon let him struggle for a few minutes. Then he lost patience and said: 'It's no use. There's no wife for you.' So the brother went home.

Next day the middle brother tried his luck. He too met the dragon, but fared no better than his big brother.

Father was very sad. It looked as if he was stuck with three big, hungry, useless boys for ever. He didn't even bother to tell Ivashko to look for a wife. But Ivashko was tired of idling at home. He thought he would like to make a life of his own, and at last his father agreed—but without much hope—that he too should go and look for a wife.

Ivashko wandered along and met the dragon. 'Where are you going, my fine lad?' said the dragon. Ivashko replied: 'My big brothers

couldn't find themselves wives, so
I thought I'd have a go.'

'Come with me,' said the
dragon. He took Ivashko and
showed him the great stone. The
boy put his shoulder to the rock
and heaved, and it rolled over
quite easily. There was a deep
black hole, and a long rope of
leather hung down into the
darkness.

'Take hold of the rope,' said
the dragon. 'I will lower you to the
bottom, and then you will see what
you will see.'

So Ivashko went down the
hole, a hundred feet, or yards, or
maybe a mile, and when he
reached the bottom he found
himself in a very fine country. He
began walking and in time came to
the Copper Kingdom. There he
met a very beautiful maiden.
'Welcome, young man,' she said.
'Sit down and tell me about yourself.'

'Where I come from, food comes before questions,' said Ivashko. The maiden smiled and gave him every kind of rich food and wine to drink with it, and he feasted heartily. When he was full, he said: 'Now I can tell you that I am looking for a wife. I have looked all over my own village, but there is no one nearly as lovely as you are. Will you be my bride?'

'Don't be too hasty,' said the maiden. 'Look around the market before you choose your bargain. You will surely find someone much more beautiful than I.' So she sent him on his way.

In time he came to the Silver Kingdom. There, sure enough, he found a girl who shone more brightly than the maiden of the Copper Kingdom as the moon outshines the stars. She too gave Ivashko fine food, and before he had finished eating he was sure that he was over ears in love with her. When he asked her to marry him, she laughed and said: 'Get along with you, lad. You have much to learn about women. Go on and look further.'

So Ivashko walked on, and in a day, or a week, or a year, he came to the Kingdom of Gold, and there he saw the loveliest of maidens. She was the sun to the silver maiden's moon. She fed the boy well, and he ate heartily because he had travelled far. Afterwards he fell on his knees before her and begged her to be his wife. 'Why not,' she said. 'You will suit me very well. I have been long enough in this kingdom, and I have a fancy to see Russia.'

Ivashko and his golden maiden began the long journey back. On the way they passed through the Silver Kingdom, and the silver maiden decided to go with them. In the Copper Kingdom that maiden, too, thought that she would throw in her lot with them. So Ivashko and three lovely girls came at last to the bottom of the hole. The rope still hung down, and far away up in the sunshine at the top Ivashko saw his two brothers who had come to look for him.

Ivashko first tied the copper maiden to the rope and the brothers pulled her up. Next it was the turn of the silver maiden. When she was safely at the top Ivashko tied the golden maiden on securely, and the brothers soon had her on firm ground.

Now Ivashko himself took hold of the rope and the brothers heaved.

When he was halfway up the brothers said to one another: 'Do we really want Ivashko to come home with us and spoil everything? Surely we would be much better off without him.' So they cut the rope, and Ivashko fell to the bottom again.

Well now, that seemed a poor reward for all he had done in finding three lovely brides. He lay there, weeping bitterly. Then he said to himself: 'There's no help for it. I can't lie down here for the rest of my days.' So he gave himself a shake and started walking.

After a while he came upon a tiny man. He came barely up to Ivashko's knee but his beard was twice his own height. Ivashko told him of his plight. 'I'd like to help you,' said the little man, 'but as you see I am not so very big and not quite as strong as I should like. However, carry on along this road and you will come to a house. There you will find a man who is somewhat taller than I, and I dare say he will help you.'

The long man proved to be indeed somewhat taller than the dwarf, for Ivashko's head came just up to his knee. 'Excuse me, sir,' said Ivashko a little nervously. 'Can you help me to get home to Russia?'

'I don't remember asking you to come here,' said the giant crossly. 'It's the same with all you Russians. You come here without an invitation and then want help to get back again. However, I suppose I must do what I can. Go on this way until you come to thirty lakes. Just beyond the last lake you will find a hut standing on chicken's legs. That is where Baba Yaga lives. I dare say she will do something for you, if she is in a good mood. If not, you will be sorry you came here in the first place.'

On Ivashko went, a long and weary walk, until he came to the hut on chicken's legs. Baba Yaga the witch saw him coming. 'What a nasty smell of Russian!' she said. 'What do you want with me, boy?'

'Excuse me, grandma,' said Ivashko. 'The long man thought you might help me to get home.'

'I might, and then again I might not,' said Baba Yaga. 'You will have to see if my eagle is willing to help. He doesn't take kindly to everyone, and he has a habit of pecking if he is displeased. Take plenty of meat with you. Flying makes him hungry, and if you can't feed him he may feed on you.'

So, after all his journeying, Ivashko reached the eagle, and a very big bird he was too. Happily he was in a good mood, and the young man clambered on to his back and settled down between the great wings. The eagle took off and flew strongly. Soon he turned his head, and Ivashko gave him a chunk of meat. So the flight went on, Ivashko holding on desperately and giving the eagle food whenever he asked. But now the last piece of meat had gone, and they still had some way to fly. Next time the eagle turned Ivashko could only say: 'Sorry! It is all gone.' So the eagle took a bite out of his shoulder, and how it hurt! Still Ivashko hung on, and at last his home lay below and the eagle made a safe landing.

That is how Ivashko came home and took back his golden bride. You might think that he would have taken the silver and copper brides too, just to punish his brothers for what they had done to him, but that was not Ivashko's way.

Ivan's Shadow

THE old folk had three sons to care for them. Two were good lads, always busy watching their sheep in the fields. The third son—well, he was called Ivanushko and he was as useless as his brothers were useful. He spent most of his days lying on the stove, whistling and catching flies.

One day mother made dumplings and told Ivanushko to take them to his brothers for dinner. She packed them neatly in a pot, and he picked it up and ambled off, not hurrying too much for it was still early and he needed to save his strength for the rest of the day.

It was a lovely day. The sun shone brightly, and Ivan's shadow moved along at his side. After a while he noticed this, and he thought to himself in his dim way: 'Who is this fellow? I don't know him. I wonder why he sticks so close. Perhaps the poor lad is hungry. Here, have a dumpling.' He tossed one at the shadow, but it kept going beside him. He threw it more dumplings. Still it didn't go away. 'What a pig!' thought Ivan, and gave it the rest of his load. Still it followed him, and in disgust Ivan threw the pot at it and it smashed to pieces.

When he got to his brothers they said: 'Where's our dinner?'

'Well, brothers, I was bringing it, but some stranger followed me and kept asking for food, so in the end he had the lot.'

'What stranger?'

'Why, this black fellow. See, he's still by my side.'

The brothers fell into a rage and gave Ivanushko a fearful beating. He went home as puzzled as he was hurt. Whoever could that black man be?

Another time, when it was coming up to Christmas, Ivan's parents sent him to town in a cart to buy what was needed for the feast. Ivan set off, cracking his whip proudly and singing a cheerful song. He had a fine time in the market, buying all sorts of things: different kinds of food, cups and plates and knives, and a big table.

It made a heavy load. On the way home the old horse began to labour under the weight and wheezed and panted. 'Poor Dobbin!' thought Ivan. 'How can I help him? I know; that table has as many legs

as the horse. It can surely make its own way home.' So he threw the table out into the road and drove on.

There were many birds, flying low over the cart and calling in their high voices. 'Poor things,' said Ivan to nimself. 'They must be starving.' He stopped the cart, got down and laid out plates in the road. He piled these high with food, and shouted: 'Eat up, little ones; you deserve Christmas just as much as us.' And he cracked his whip and set the horse going again.

The road ran through a plantation of young trees. There had been a fire and many of the trees were burnt down to stumps. 'Oh dear!' thought Ivan. 'Those little fellows have no hats. They will catch cold, as sure as my name's whatever it is.' Again he stopped, and covered as many stumps as he could with cups and pots.

Ivan was feeling very happy. He had done many good deeds already that day and he longed to do more. When he came to a stream he thought he would give the old horse a treat, so he took the beast out of the shafts and led him to the water for a drink. The horse was not thirsty and took no notice. 'What's the matter? Don't you like the taste?' said Ivan. 'Perhaps you would rather have salt with it.' He took out the big bag he had bought and poured the lot into the stream. Still the horse would not drink. 'Drink, you selfish old bag-of-bones!' shouted Ivan angrily, and he picked up the branch of a tree and hit the horse on the head with it. The old horse just dropped dead.

Ivan looked in the cart. Of all the goods he had bought in the town only a bag of spoons was left. He picked up the bag and slung it over his shoulder, and began to walk the rest of the way home. As he lumbered on his way the spoons rattled against one another, making a chattering noise. To Ivanushko it sounded as if the spoons were saying 'Silly Ivan! Silly Ivan!'

'So that's what you think,' he shouted in a temper. He flung the bag

on the ground and jumped on it, screaming: 'That will teach you to be rude.'

The family were waiting for him when he got home. 'Where's everything?' they said. 'Hasn't the table got here yet?' asked Ivan. 'I left it on the road and was sure it would get home first. The birds are using the plates. I left the cups and pots for those poor hatless trees. The old horse wanted the salt to flavour the water, and as for the spoons they didn't deserve to be carried so I left them to take care of themselves.'

'Where is the horse?'

'He had a headache, so I had to leave him behind with the cart.'

The brothers could put up with their little brother no longer. They talked about what they should do with Ivan, and decided that they must get rid of him once and for all. One day when he was dozing by the stove they grabbed hold of him and stuffed him into a sack. They carried him to the river. It was frozen hard, so they left him on the bank while they went to look for a hole in the ice. After a while Ivan heard the jingling of harness, and a rich man came by in his fine horse-sleigh. Ivan began to struggle in his sack, shouting 'I won't do it! I won't do it!'

'What won't you do?' asked the rich man.

'They are going to make me governor of a province, and I don't want it. What do I know about ruling and handing out justice?'

'I know all about that,' said the rich man. 'I wouldn't mind being a governor. We had better change places.'

He let Ivanushko out of the sack and crawled in himself. Ivan tied it tightly. Then he took the sleigh and cracked his whip, and away went the three big horses. Soon the brothers came back and picked up the sack. They carried it, puffing and panting, until they came to a hole. They dropped their burden through the ice, and it went: 'Bubble! Bubble!' out of sight.

The brothers started homeward, half glad to be rid of their tiresome brother, half ashamed of what they had done. There was a jingling sound, and along came Ivanushko, cracking his whip and singing at the top of his voice. 'What do you think of my river horses?' he shouted. 'They are the pick of the underwater stable. Gee up, my beauties!' And they watched him out of sight.

Prince Ivan and the Undying

WHEN Prince Ivan was a baby his nurse used to rock him to sleep in his cradle, and every night she sang this lullaby:
'*Over the seas*
In a far distant land
Vasilisa waits
For our prince to take her hand.'

Years passed. Ivan was fifteen, a tall, strong young man. He went to his father on the day after his birthday, and said:

'Father, it is time for me to go in search of my bride.'

The king was surprised. 'What bride, my son?' he said. 'You know nothing of brides or of the world beyond the palace gardens.'

'When I was a baby,' the young prince said, 'my nurse used to sing to me, and I have always remembered the words:

"*Over the seas*
In a far distant land
Vasilisa waits
For our prince to take her hand."

Vasilisa has been waiting too long. It is time I went to claim her.'

This was a wise king. He had no wish to stand in his son's way, and he saw how determined the young man was. So he gave the lad his blessing, and sent messages to every corner of the kingdom, saying that it was the duty of every man to aid the prince in his quest.

So Prince Ivan's journey began. He began it, having no idea which way to go and trusting that the old nursery song would somehow guide him to his bride.

He stopped for the night in a town, and in the morning went for a walk in the streets, thinking about his quest. In the market place he saw a man tied to the whipping-post and the hangman lashing his bare back. He asked one of the people watching: 'What has the man done?'

'He is a debtor. He borrowed five hundred pounds from a money-lender, and now the time is up and he can't pay.'

'Can he not find a friend to put up the money for him?' asked the prince.

'They are all afraid. A soothsayer has said that if anyone helps him his wife will be stolen away by Koshchey the Undying.'

The prince walked on, deeply troubled by what he had seen and heard. Should he not go to the wretched man's help? He could well afford the money, and as for the wife, he didn't have one to be stolen. He made up his mind quickly and hurried back to the market place, where he handed over the money and walked away before the man could be untied.

He heard the sound of running feet behind him and turned. It was the man he had saved. The man knelt down and gave thanks to the prince. Then he arose and said: 'You will not regret this kindness. I will serve you to the end of time.'

The prince clasped his hand, and the man said: 'My first service will be to find your bride.'

'How shall I call you?'

'I am Bulat.'

The Prince got a horse for his companion, and they rode on together. They rode for a week, or a month, or a year, and came at length to the remote kingdom where Vasilisa's father was king.

'Now for your wooing,' said Bulat. 'Go to the cooks and order them to prepare their finest birds for your use, chicken, duck and goose, and have them ready.'

Vasilisa sat high in her golden tower, dreaming of her lover to come. Bulat stood below and threw a stone. It broke the vane on top of the tower and the princess was alarmed. Then Bulat ran back to Prince Ivan and said: 'Quick! Give me a wing of the chicken.' He took it and ran to the tower again. Kneeling before the princess Bulat said: 'Greetings! Prince Ivan sends you honourable words and begs you to accept this bird.'

Vasilisa was still scared of the intruder and said not a word. So Bulat answered for her: 'Thank you, Bulat. And thanks to Prince Ivan too. Now, will you take a glass of vodka with me?'

He returned to the prince and said: 'Now for the duck.' He took a wing and ran back, again offering food to Vasilisa. Again she sat silently, and he had to speak for her: 'Thank you, Bulat. And my thanks to Prince Ivan for his kind gift. Now will you take a glass of vodka?'

Bulat hurried back. 'Quick! It is going well. Now it is the turn of the goose.' He took a wing and offered it to the princess. She had by now got over her fright. She greeted the messenger kindly and got up to pour him a glass of vodka. When she handed it to him, he seized her by the hand and forced her to follow him out of the tower. Then he put her on a horse, raced back to the prince, and they rode quickly away, carrying the princess with them.

They rode hard all that day and on through the night. By then Vasilisa's city was far behind, but Bulat knew that the princess's father would not give up his daughter without a struggle. Already many soldiers must be on their trail. He said to the prince: 'I must go back. I have left my ring behind. Go on and I will catch you up shortly.'

'What does a ring matter? I will give you half a dozen.'

'My ring is beyond price. It was my mother's farewell gift.'

Bulat turned back, and met the pursuers in a narrow pass. There he slew them all, but for a single man whom he ordered to take news of the battle to the king. He soon caught up with Prince Ivan, and they continued their flight. Bulat still did not believe that the king would give up, so he pretended to have lost a priceless handkerchief and turned back to find it. Again he met an armed party and cut them down to the last man.

'Did you find your handkerchief?' asked the prince, who knew very well what Bulat had been doing for his sake.

'Yes, I have it here.'

On they went, but now they were getting very weary and night was fast coming on. So they made camp for the night. Prince Ivan kept the first watch while Bulat slept. The prince marched up and down, but he just could not keep his eyes open and soon he was fast asleep. In the darkest part of the night the air suddenly turned icy cold, and Koshchey the Undying came to the camp, a dreadful sight. He stepped over Prince Ivan and Bulat and took up Vasilisa in his arms.

In the light of dawn Ivan awoke and discovered that his bride was gone. He broke into an agony of tears, and the noise of his grief awoke Bulat.

'What is your trouble?'

'Vasilisa is gone.'

'I knew what would happen if you failed to keep watch. That horrible old bonebag Koshchey has done it. Now we shall have to go after him.'

On they rode, for a day or a week, and came to the land where Koshchey ruled. Then they took off their fine clothes and disguised themselves as shepherds. In this way they were able to come to Koshchey's castle without being detected.

Now Vasilisa had not become Koshchey's slave. Indeed he was a little afraid of her because she was a princess. He let her do as she wished as long as she did not leave the castle, and it had become her habit to bathe each morning in the milk of goats.

On the morning that the prince and Bulat arrived the maid who milked the goats was carrying her bucket into the palace. The pretended shepherds came and teased her. While they were talking Prince Ivan tossed a gold ring into the bucket, and it was so full that the girl could not fish it out. She carried the bucket to the princess's room and said: 'I am sorry, madam. One of those rogues of shepherds threw something into the milk and I can't reach it.'

'Never mind. I will strain the milk before I have my bath.'

When Vasilisa saw the ring she knew it for one which she had herself given to the prince during their flight. She ordered the shepherds to be brought before her. They came. 'Greetings, princess,' said Bulat. 'It is time for that glass of vodka?'

She laughed, and Ivan took her in his arms. 'Did you think to escape me so easily?' he said. 'Even if you had been taken into the depth of the sea or up to the highest cloud, I would have followed.'

So they were happy together for a while. Then it was time for Koshchey to return. Bulat said: 'We must find out where Koshchey's weakness lies. No man is Undying. Ask him what his secret is. Where does he hide his life that no man can take it?'

Vasilisa did not want to be left alone with the Undying, so Ivan and Bulat hid themselves where they could see and hear all that went on. They had only just gone into hiding when Koshchey came home from hunting. He was in a bad mood. 'What a stink!' he said. 'It is many a day since I last smelt a Russian but I surely smell one now. Where is the scoundrel?'

'Come, come, my love,' said Vasilisa. 'You have spent so long in Russia lately that it has got right into your nose. Get rid of these fancies and come to dinner.'

So they ate, and afterwards Koshchey rested from his hunting. Vasilisa sat beside him and fondled his hideous cheeks. 'What a day it has been!' she said. 'I could not rest for fear that you might have come to some harm. There are wild animals in the forest, and any one of them might have slain you.'

Koshchey roared with laughter. 'Why, you little fool, I fear no wild thing in the world, beast or man.'

'How can that be, my love?' said Vasilisa. 'Where do you keep your life safe?'

'Why, in that old broom that stands by the door.'

As soon as Koshchey went away Vasilisa went to Prince Ivan. 'He says that he keeps his life in the broom.'

'Nonsense,' said Bulat. 'He is trying to fool you. You must find some other way to get his secret.'

Vasilisa had a good idea. She took the old broom and dressed it up in silks and ribbons. Then she laid it on cushions on the table.

'What in the name of all the devils is that?' asked Koshchey roughly, when he returned.

'I couldn't leave your life standing at the door,' said Vasilisa. 'I had to take care of it properly.'

'You are a dear little fool,' said Koshchey fondly. 'Did you really believe that my life was in a broom? No, it is in the goat that gives you your milk every day.'

While Koshchey was hunting Vasilisa took the goat into the castle and decorated it with golden bells and painted its horns with gold. Koshchey laughed and laughed when he saw it. 'I never knew such a woman,' he said. 'Who would keep his life in an old nanny-goat? No, my life is not so easily found. Far away over the sea there is an island. On that island grows a tree. Under that tree a bronze casket lies buried. Inside that casket there lurks a fox. Inside the fox there is a duck. Inside the duck there is an egg. That egg holds my life. It is safe enough there, my dear.'

As soon as Koshchey had gone hunting next morning, Prince Ivan and Bulat went in search of the island. It was a long journey, and even before they had reached the coast they ran out of food and became weak with hunger. They came upon a bitch feeding her pups, and Bulat wanted to kill her for the sake of the little meat there was on her bones. The bitch said: 'Don't kill me and leave my babies motherless. I would make a poor meal, but alive I may be useful to you.'

So they let her live and went on their weary way. On a rock an eagle sat, nursing her young. Bulat put an arrow to his bow and took aim. 'Don't kill me and leave my babies motherless,' said the eagle. 'Let me live to serve you.' So they left her alone.

Now the great ocean lay before them. They came to the shore and saw a big fat fish swimming in the shallows with her young ones around her. 'At last,' said Bulat, 'here is something worth eating.' He took his spear, but the fish called out: 'Don't kill me and leave my children motherless. I would be good to eat, but living I would be even better.'

'Let it be so,' said Bulat, and he and Prince Ivan sat down beside the sea and tried to forget their hunger. There was a fisherman out at sea, and they waved to him to come, and bargained with him to sail them to the island. So at last they reached their goal.

On the island grew a single great tree. Bulat took it in his strong hands, and with a mighty heave he tore it out by the roots. It left a big hole, and at the bottom they found a casket of bronze. Bulat climbed down and lifted it to the surface. The prince forced the lid, and out shot a fox. It ran away at a great pace.

'Oh,' said the prince, 'if only we had that bitch to chase it.'

At once the bitch appeared. She raced after the fox and brought it down. Then with a slash of her sharp teeth she tore it open. Out came a duck and flapped away over their heads.

'We could do with that eagle now,' said Prince Ivan.

They heard a whistling in the air, and the eagle stooped, taking the duck in her great talons. The power of the eagle's dive had taken them both out to sea, and as the duck died it dropped an egg into the water.

'Fish, oh fish!' called the prince. 'Where are you?'

The water by the shore became calm for a moment and the fish appeared. She was carrying the egg in her mouth, and she laid it gently on the sand. The prince picked it up very carefully and put it into his saddlebag. Then they began the journey back to Koshchey's castle.

Koshchey had just got back from the hunt. As he climbed down from his horse Prince Ivan stepped forward and threw the egg. It struck the giant right on the forehead, and he fell dead.

And that, you might say, was the end of the story. Prince Ivan and Bulat and the beautiful Princess Vasilisa were to have many more

adventures before they came home to the prince's father's kingdom, but for the prince and his bride all dangers were as nothing because they were no longer apart.

They came home at last and were married, and who do you think was the honoured guest at their wedding? Why, Bulat of course. Without him the prince would not have found his princess, and Koshchey would have been for ever the Undying.

Y OUNG Ivan was not the brightest of boys. He lay on the stove all day while his brothers went dashing around, doing things. He had plenty of time for thinking, and so he had very many stories stored up in his head. In the dark winter evenings he used to tell these to his family, making them forget for a while the harsh cold outside and the hard toil awaiting them in the morning.

This is one of Ivan's tales.

There was a mother goat who had made herself a hut in the forest. There she lived in safety with her family of fine kids. Every day she went out foraging for food. Before she left she took care to bolt the door with her children safe inside. On her return she would knock on the door and sing:

> *'Now, my babies, open the door.*
> *I have eaten fresh grass from the forest floor.*
> *Spring water is making my udders burst;*
> *Open wide, let me in, and quench your thirst.'*

The kids would let her in, and then she fed them well. So it would go on. Every time she went out she would shut them in very carefully.

There was a big grey wolf living nearby, and he used to watch what the mother goat did. One day, when she was out of sight, he went to the hut and rapped on the door with his big hairy paw. Then he called out in his harsh voice:

> *'Hey, you kids,*
> *Open wide.*
> *Your mother wants*
> *To come inside.'*

The kids said to one another: 'That is not our mother's voice. She sings us quite a different tune.' So they refused to open the door, and the wolf went away growling and lashing his tail.

Before long the mother goat was back. She rapped on the door with her hard hoof and sang:

'*Now, my babies, open the door.*
I have eaten fresh grass from the forest floor.
Spring water is making my udders burst;
Open wide, let me in, and quench your thirst.'

'That is mother's voice; that is mother's tune,' said the kids. They hastened to let her in and told her that the wolf had been after them.

Next morning, when the mother goat left her children she told them never to open the door except when they heard her voice and her usual words.

But the wolf had been listening, hidden among the trees, and very soon he was at the door. He tapped with stone to imitate the sound of the goat's hoof, and sang in the softest voice he could manage:

'Now my babies, open the door.
I have eaten fresh grass from the forest floor.
Spring water is making my udders burst;
Open wide, let me in, and quench your thirst.'

The kids threw open the door. In bounded the wolf. He chased those kids around the hut and swallowed them all, one by one. Only the youngest managed to take refuge in the empty stove.

Home came the mother goat. She sang her usual song, but no one came running to let her in. She pushed the door and it swung open, but no little kids were to be seen. She sat down weeping. Then she heard a little squeaking sound from the stove. She looked inside and there was her smallest baby.

He told his mother the whole sad story. When she heard it she was filled with sorrow. Throwing herself on the ground she sang sadly:

'Dear babies, why
Did we have to part?
The wolf slew you all
And darkened my heart.'

'Oh come, neighbour,' said the wolf, coming through the open door. 'How could you think so ill of me? Let us go for a walk and talk together as good neighbours ought.'

'I have no heart for walking or talking,' said the goat sadly.

'Don't say that,' said the wolf, and he went on pleading until she had to give in.

So they went side by side through the forest. They came to a clearing where the woodmen had been at work. They had dug a pit and filled it with sticks to make a fire on which they would cook their dinner. The fire still smoked and threw out great heat.

'Let us have a game,' said the wolf. 'That will cheer you up. We will take it in turns to jump over the pit, and the one who jumps farthest will be the winner.'

He went first. He took a short run and jumped as hard as he could, but the kids lay heavy inside him and he fell short. Down on the hot embers he came. Splllt! went the tight skin of his belly. It split wide open, and out ran all the little kids, for he had swallowed them whole.

What a happy moment that was! The mother goat led them home, rejoicing. From that day the kids opened the door only to their mother's voice, until they too grew big and strong and could go by themselves to eat the forest grass and drink the spring water.

Can You Hear Me?

THREE brothers went into the forest to cut wood. They took an iron pot with them and a handful of gruel for their dinner. All morning they chopped and trimmed, and by noon they were all very hungry.

'Time for dinner,' said the eldest; so they built a fire and put the pot on it.

'How do we light the fire?'

'You know that beekeeper's cottage we passed. The beekeeper will surely let us have a light.'

So the eldest brother went to the cottage and said: 'Grandad, will you give us a light for our fire?'

'Yes, if you will sing me a song.'

'I can't sing.'

'Then do a little dance.'

'I'm no good at dancing.'

'No fire for you then,' said the old man, and he picked up a stick and gave the eldest brother such a whack on the back that it took the skin off.

The second brother tried next, but he did no better. He too came away with no fire and with little skin to his back.

'Now what do we do?' said the two brothers. Simple Ivan, the youngest, said: 'You haven't got very far, have you? For all you are so clever. Let us see what the daftie can do!' And he went to the cottage.

'Give us a light, Grandad,' he said.

'First let me see you dance.'

'Can't dance, Grandad.'

'Tell me a tale, then.'

'That I will,' said Ivan, and he sat down and got comfortable. 'Now you watch out, Grandad. If you interrupt me, I'll serve you as you served my big brothers and take the skin off your back.'

The old beekeeper said not a word but settled himself with his bald head gleaming in the sun.

'Can you hear me?' said Ivan.

'I can hear you.'

76

'Well,' said Ivan, 'once I had a horse and I rode it to the forest to cut wood. I jogged along with my axe stuck in my belt. Jog, jog, we went, and I bobbed up and down, and the axe went thump, thump, against my horse's rump. Thump it went and thump again until it cut off the horse's backside. Can you hear me?' said Ivan, and he slapped the old man on his bald head with his glove.

'I can hear you, my lad.'

'I rode for about three years on what was left of the horse, and then in a field I saw my horse's rump. There it was, eating grass as calm as calm. I caught it and sewed it back on the front of my horse. Then we rode on for another three years. Can you hear me?' said Ivan, and he slapped the bald head with his glove.

'I can hear you.'

'I rode on and on until I came to a forest. There stood a big oak tree. I climbed up it for a week or two until I got to heaven. There I found fine cows for sale, very cheap, but the price of flies was something shocking. So I climbed down again and collected a sackful of flies and went back again. For every fly I got one cow and its calf in exchange. When all my flies were gone I drove my cows—a herd of a thousand or so—back to the place where I had got into heaven. But do you know? Some fool on earth had cut down the oak tree. I did the only thing I could think of: I killed all my fine cows and cut their hides into strips to make a rope. I tied one end to the heavenly gates and climbed down. What a climb that was. When I reached the end of the rope I was short by a few feet, just about the height of your house, Grandad. Can you hear me?' And Ivan slapped the old man's bald head with his glove.

'I can hear you.'

'I was scared, I can tell you. I daren't jump. However, a peasant down below was mowing a field, and some of the grass blew into the air. I caught it and plaited it into a rope. I was just ready to finish my climb when the wind got up. It began to swing me around. Now I was over Moscow, now Petersburg was below. Scared stiff I was. Then the rope broke and I fell into a bog. I sank up to my neck and couldn't move an inch. A duck made its nest on my head and laid a clutch of eggs. Then a wolf came to eat the eggs. I just managed to grab it by the tail, and it dragged me out of the mud. Can you hear me, Grandad?' And Ivan slapped the old man on his bald head again.

'I can hear you.'

Ivan was getting desperate. He couldn't think of any more nonsense to add to his tale, and still the old man had not interrupted him. So he had to start again.

'Once upon a time my grandfather was riding on your grandfather . . .'

'That's not true,' interrupted the old man. 'It was my grandfather who rode on your grandfather.'

'Aha!' shouted Ivan. 'Caught you!' And he picked up the stick and gave the beekeeper three cuts, one for each of his brothers and one for himself. Then he helped himself to some burning sticks from the fire and went back to his brothers. They lit the fire and put gruel on to cook.

When it's cooked I'll go on with this story. For the time being this is

THE END